SIMPLE SONGS FOR SLIM SUNDAYS

COMPILED BY
JOSEPH M. MARTIN

Harold Flammer
MUSIC

EXCLUSIVELY DISTRIBUTED BY

HAL•LEONARD®
CORPORATION

7777 W. BLUEMOUND RD. P.O. BOX 13819 MILWAUKEE, WI 53213

Visit Shawnee Press Online at **www.shawneepress.com**

FOREWORD

There is a special art to creating dynamic and effective anthems with a limited amount of material. The goal of this present collection is to provide quality musical moments within the technical boundaries of the average church choir. Some of our most celebrated writers have contributed to the effort and we hope the results will be an encouragement to choirs.

Contained in these pages are general use anthems for almost any occasion that can be learned and presented with a minimal amount of preparation time. Tender songs of reflection join with soaring anthems of worship and praise to create one of the most useful compilations we have ever produced. Made up of best-sellers and proven winners from our Shawnee Select archives, these simple but effective pieces will be used again and again. It is our hope that these sacred chorals will become essential repertoire for your worship planning. Enjoy!

Joseph M. Martin

COME, LET US JOIN

for two-part mixed voices, accompanied

Words by
ISAAC WATTS

Music by
JOSEPH M. MARTIN (BMI)

* Optional: Men sing melody alone until middle of m. 12.

4

8

10

for Connie

CAST THY BURDEN UPON THE LORD

for S.A.B. voices*, accompanied

Psalm 55:22
Adapted by B.H.

Music by
BENJAMIN HARLAN
(ASCAP)

* Also published for S.A.T.B. voices (Code No. A-6520)

car-ry you and sus - tain＿ you.＿＿＿ Cast thy bur-den up-on the

Lord.

SOP. *mf*
ALTO

Cast thy bur - den up - on the＿ Lord, cast thy bur - den up-

BAR. *mf*

on the Lord, cast thy bur-den up-on the Lord. He will not

fail you. He'll walk be-side you. He'll e-ven car-ry you and sus-

tain you. *mf* *(unis.)* Cast thy bur-den up-on the

COME, THOU FOUNT OF EVERY BLESSING

for 2- Part mixed voices, accompanied

Tune: NETTLETON

Words by
ROBERT ROBINSON (1735-1790)

Arranged by
HAL HOPSON (ASCAP)

20

sought me when a stran - ger, Wan-d'ring from the fold of

He sought me when a stran - ger, When wan-d'ring far from

God; He, to res - cue me from dan - ger, In - ter -

God; He res - cued me from dan - ger, He res - cued

posed His pre - cious blood.

me by His own pre - cious blood.

22

CONSIDER THE LILIES

for S.A.B. voices, accompanied

Words by
J. PAUL WILLIAMS (ASCAP)

Music by
JAMES M. STEVENS (ASCAP)

30

IN EVERY LAND BEGIN THE SONG

for S.A.B. voices, accompanied*

Words by
J. PAUL WILLIAMS (ASCAP)

Music by
JOSEPH M. MARTIN (BMI)

* Orchestration: LB5606
CD Track (with demo): MD5092

gin___ the song, let al - le - lu - ias fill the air. Sing praise to whom all

praise be - longs, a song___ of joy___ de - clare. God's

love,_____ God's love,_____

(unis.) God's love all love ex - cel - ling, God's love is

34

THINK ON THESE THINGS

for 2-Part mixed voices, accompanied

Music by
RON SPRUNGER

PHILIPPIANS 4: 8-9

INTRODUCTION (optional);

The Apostle Paul wrote to the people at Philippi to encourage them. His words were: "Finally, brothers,* whatever is true, whatever is noble, whatever is right, whatever is pure, whatever is lovely, whatever is admirable - if anything is excellent or praiseworthy - think on such things." This song will help us remember his important words.

* or *brothers and sisters,*

42

PEACE LIKE A RIVER/AMEN!

for 2-Part mixed voices, accompanied

TRADITIONAL
Arranged by
DOUGLAS E. WAGNER (ASCAP)

48

COME WITH SHOUTING

for S.A.B. voices, accompanied

Words by
J. PAUL WILLIAMS (ASCAP)
based on Isaiah 35

Music by
DOUGLAS NOLAN (BMI)

52

Lift up your praise to the Lord! Praise the Lord! Chil-dren re-joice and shout!

Clap your hands! Come, ye chil - dren of Je - ru - sa - lem.

(div.)   (unis.)

rit.   Slower (♩ = ca. 96)

Slower (♩ = ca. 96)
legatissimo

dim.   rit.

WALK ALONG BESIDE ME,
O MY LORD

for S.A.B. voices, accompanied

Words and Music by
DON BESIG (ASCAP)

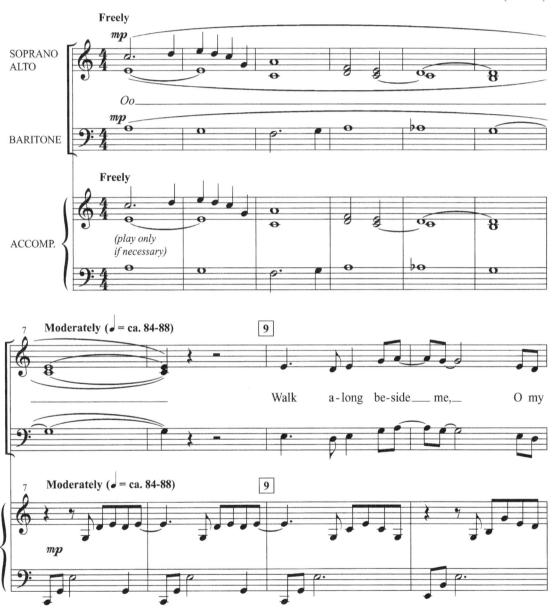

Lord._____ Lead me on ev-'ry step of the way_____ and

help me find the joy in each__ new day.__ Take my life and

Oo,_____

use it,__ O my Lord._____ Help me find and help me share__

oo_____

the gifts You have giv-en, gifts so rare.__

Build my faith and watch me from a-bove.__

Guide me pa-tient-ly__ and teach me__ how to

* No breath here.

60

62

and wak-en me a-gain to see____ the light___ of a

new to-mor-row, the peace I'm search-ing

for. Walk a-long be-side me, O my Lord.

WE BRING OUR THANKS

for S.A.B. voices, accompanied

Words by
J. PAUL WILLIAMS (ASCAP)

Music by
RUTH ELAINE SCHRAM (ASCAP)

we bring our thanks to You._____ For ev-'ry good and per-fect

gift is from a-bove, sent to the earth from the

Fa - ther with love. He free-ly gives of His

68

SING FOREVER TO THE LORD

for S.A.B. voices, accompanied

JON PAIGE (BMI)

D 5430

74

for the Park Methodist Church Choir
A CLOSING PRAYER
(S.A.B. and Piano)

by Don Besig

Performance time: approx. 2:35 (2:55)

Copyright © 1978, 1980, Harold Flammer Music
A Division of Shawnee Press, Inc.
Sole Selling Agent For This Arrangement: SHAWNEE PRESS, Inc., Nashville, TN 37212
International Copyright Secured   Made In U.S.A.   All Rights Reserved

80

82

*No breath